I0152708

Leadership Principles for Teens

"Empowering student to be Future-Ready"

Empowering students to be Future-Ready"

Reba Haley, Ph.D.
P.O Box 648
Valrico, Florida 33595

Library of Congress cataloging in publication
data Haley, Reba Library of Congress
Insight Consulting International Group, Inc.
Website; icigroupintl.org
Email; icigintl@gmail.com
Email; drrebahaley@outlook.com

Leadership Principles for Teens
"Empowering students to be Future-Ready"

978-0-9646594-9-0

Empowering students to be Future-Ready"

TABLE OF CONTENTS

Introduction   5

Chapter 1 Social and Workplace Etiquettes   10

Chapter 2 Practical Leadership Principles   14

Chapter 3 Life Skills for Student Success   22

Chapter 4 Financial Literacy for Career Success   29

Chapter 5 Risk Factors of E-Cigarettes & Drugs   44

Chapter 6 Business Principles for Success   50

Chapter 7 Self-Care Practices & Routines   56

Chapter 8 Impact of Substance Abuse on Families   62

Conclusion   81

Bibliography   84

About the Author   86

Empowering students to be Future-Ready"

INTRODUCTION

*The Leadership Principles for Teens —
Empowering students to be Future-Ready* contains
principles, methods, strategies, and tips to
keep students from dropping out of school
and take control of their lives. The life skills
and wide range of subjects can help students
thrive in the classroom and in the world
beyond. The author was a former high-school
drop-out who was sent to a juvenile detention
facility for truancy and placed in foster care
after her parents divorced.

Dr. Reba returned to school and
completed her GED and continued her
education to obtain a medical assistant
certificate. She furthered her education and
graduated from college with an associate
degree, bachelor degree, master degree and
doctorate degree. Dr. Haley is a mother, wife,
business owner, author, educator, ordained
minister, therapist and certified addiction
professional with years of experience working
with youth and adults with mental health and
substance use disorders.

Since, the coronavirus students faced
loneliness and anxiety to severe or suicidal
depression. Prior, to COVID-19 the research

Empowering students to be Future-Ready" and statistics of teenage highschool drop-out rates, juvenile delinquency cases, and suicide were alarming. "In the United States over 1.2 million students drop out of high school. That's a student every26 seconds, or 7,000 a day according to the Department of Education. The lack of education then leads to a lack of opportunities for employment and increases the risk of incarceration." Of all males in federal and stateprisons, 80 percent do not have a high school diploma. There is a direct correlation with a lack of high school education and incarceration.

One in ten male dropouts between the ages of 16 and 24 is either in prison or in juvenile detention. "An African-American man without his high school diploma will be imprisoned by his mid-thirties. It is further noted that juvenile incarceration decreases the likelihood of high school graduation by 13 percent" according to the Hamilton Project. The National Institute of Mental Health states that suicide is the second leading cause of death for people between the ages of 10 and 24. Research suggests that in the next 24 hours 1,439 teens will attempt suicide. If you feel suicidal you are urged to call The National Suicide Prevention Hotline at 1-800-273-8255 for help, and talk to a teacher or adult.

Empowering students to be Future-Ready"
Since, the COVID pandemic there was an increased loneliness, stress, anxiety, and depression, among students. It's okay to feel sad and lonely, but coping strategies can improve their mental health and well-being. Students that learn to practice self-care can manage stress and make their lives better. Poor choices lead to bad consequences, but good decisions lead to personal, academic, and professional success. Education is the key to lifting students out of poverty and into the middle class, or from the middle class into the upper class. If they graduate from high school, but do not wish to attend college, they must attend a vocational or trade school in order to avoid poverty and improve their quality of life.

Leadership Principles for Teens, " *Empowering students to be Future-Ready"* contains principles, techniques, and methods that were developed over many lectures and training sessions. The leadership principles prepare students to be peer leaders and to be future leaders in adulthood. The techniques contain principles to manage conflicts, solve problems, eliminate vaping, and avoid bullying behaviors. The goals are to equip students with life skills to improve their academic, personal, and professional lives.

Empowering students to be Future-Ready"

Chapter 1 details school, work, social manners, and etiquette that can build confidence and help teens navigate life. Students learn how to build social and emotion learning skills for academic and personal success. In Chapter 2 the leadership principles show students how to positively influence others and become leaders. Chapter 3 offers techniques on life skills for student success and skills on how to control (self-regulate) emotions and evade bullying behaviors and handle conflicts non-violently. The skills help improve emotional learning and increase empathy.

In Chapter 4 the financial and business principles can promote financial literacy, career success and help students avoid debt and bankruptcy as adults. Students learn the importance of credit,budgeting and saving. In Chapter 5 students learn the effects of drugs and E-cigarettes on the brain. Teens learn how to problem solve and resolve conflicts peacefully. In Chapter 6 students learn basic business principles, such as organizational managementto succeed in life. In Chapter 7 students learn how to practice self-care to reduce stress and manage life events. Chapter 8 details the effects of drug and alcohol abuse on families and family solutions.

Empowering students to be Future-Ready"

Leadership Principles for Teens —
Empowering students to be Future-Ready contains a broad array of subjects to improve decision-making, decrease vaping, and increase high-school graduation rates. Students learn to achieve in the classroom and in the world. The author's goals are to help students overcome obstacles in school and in life so that they can thrive and succeed. She travels and gives presentations to educators and students. She has written a basic life skills book to help students thrive in the classroom and beyond. The author's mentoring program prepares students to say yes to their dreams, education, and goals while saying no to harmful choices. The best gift a student can give themselves is the ability to make better decisions to have a successful future.

Chapter 1

Social and Workplace Etiquettes

Etiquette is a code of behavior that describes expectations for social action. Manners are needed every day to make a good impression. They should be taught at home, but some students are not learning these basic skills. The list of manners and etiquette for work and school are what everyone needs to succeed. Teens with good manners will command respect, which can help them academically, professionally and socially.

The detailed principles of etiquette cover school and social situations including dinner behavior. The manners and etiquette classes reinforce good manners and common courtesy. These are important and everyday principles that will affect students' future.

1. If someone is speaking, do not interrupt them; but wait until they are finished.
2. If it is necessary to interrupt, say *please* or *excuse me* before speaking.
3. Say "please" and "thank you."

4. Apologize when you've done something wrong.

5. Males do not touch a lady's hair without asking.
6. Cough into your elbow and cover your mouth when sneezing.
7. Ask permission to do things.
8. Brush your teeth and floss daily.
9. Females do not wear a bedroom scarf in public.
10. Remove make-up nightly.
11. Wash your sheets weekly.
12. Gentlemen open doors and pull out chairs for young ladies.
13. Make eye contact during a conversation.
14. Wash your hands after using the restroom.
15. Use sanitary pads and tampons, not toilet paper during menstruation.
16. Use deodorant daily.
17. Bathe or shower once in the morning and once at night for best hygiene.
18. Shake hands when greeting someone new.
19. Use proper table manners when eating.
20. Don't text, talk on the phone, or use social media when face to face with others.
21. Wash your hands daily.
22. Wash your dishes after eating.
23. Wash your hands before taking items from the refrigerator.

24. Wash your hands after using the restroom.
25. Don't move young men into your apartment; allow them to provide a place for you to live.
26. Don't bully or verbally, physically or emotionally abuse anyone.
27. Change undergarments daily.
28. Music played in your car should be heard only inside the car.
29. Never talk with food in your mouth.
30. Don't use your cell phone at the dinner table; ask to be excused from the table.
31. Always wash your hands before preparing or eating food.
32. Don't wear strong cologne or perfume.
33. Be on time for school.
34. Be home before dark.
35. Don't tell lies.
36. Don't skip school.
37. Don't hit or fight.
38. Don't steal.
39. Don't snatch anything.
40. Don't talk while the teacher is talking.
41. Respect all adults.
42. Don't disrespect your parents or caregivers.
43. Be grateful for your belongings.
44. Pick up your liter.
45. Don't use profanity in the presence of

your parents or an adult.
46. Be kind and treat others like you want to be treated.
47. Tip the waiter or waitress between 10 and 15%.
48. Don't date more than one person at a time.
49. Keep your word.
50. Be on time for work, interviews, school.
51. Give back to the community.
52. Listen and learn from the elders.
53. Find a mentor and grow.
54. Don't text while driving.
55. Don't text during dinner with family or friends.
56. Look for opportunities to compliment and be kind to others.

Work etiquettes are professional workplace behaviors that help you conduct yourself on the job. Employers seek employees that are punctual, neatly dressed and possess good manners. Manners and etiquettes can be learned from watching parents or other adults, or by instruction. School etiquette, good manners and social etiquette should be practiced regularly. Good manners can make a difference in your success or failure in life.

Chapter 2

Practical Leadership Principles

According to Webster's dictionary, a *leader* is *"the person who leads or commands a group, organization, or country."* A leader is a person in a group that possesses the combination of personality and leadership skills that make others want to follow his or her direction. Anyone can be a follower, but a leader motivates and inspires others to follow.

A peer leader is a student that has learned from experience and has developed skills to guide other students. A peer leader inspires others to be their best and make good choices. Teen leaders have good follow-through and they influence others. If you are a peer leader, you positively impact the lives of others.

A teen or young leader is a great communicator and has strong verbal and written skills. Teen and young leaders are good listeners and trustworthy. Leaders are not perfect, but they make good decisions. A teen leader makes decisions that are in the best interest of the team, school, and family.

Leadership Principles for Teens

A great leader possesses qualities, traits, and characteristics that unite people.

- ❖ What type of leader do I want to be?
- ❖ Do you make a positive difference in the lives of others?
- ❖ Do you need to improve your grades?
- ❖ Are you a good communicator?
- ❖ Are you a good listener and respectful of others?
- ❖ Are you a leader or follower? Do you follow others when they go against your beliefs and values?
- ❖ Do you volunteer and help others?
- ❖ What can you do to be a better student and person?

What you can do to develop a better sense of right and wrong?

_____

What improvement can you make to be a better person?

_____

The following leadership qualities and characteristics can help you become a good and caring person and effective peer leader.

Leadership Qualities and Characteristics

Effective leaders have good qualities such as intelligence and honesty. A leader is smart and knowledgeable. How are your grades? What can you do to improve your grade? Do you encourage students and peers to be the best they can be?

An exceptional peer leader inspires others, cooperative, works in groups, and with people from different genders, ethnicities and cultures. The greatness of a leader is determined by how he or she treats others. A great leader is consciously thoughtful of others. Do you make an effort to be thoughtful and considerate of others?

The golden rule or law of reciprocity is the principle of, *"treating others as one would wish to be treated."* If you do not wish to be bullied, then don't bully others. According to the dictionary, the definition of a bully is, *"a person who uses strength or power to harm or intimidate those who are weaker."*

Bullying Behaviors

➢ Teasing and making someone feel the brunt of the prank or joke.

➢ Talking down about other people to feel good about self.

➢ Using social media, text, or email as a bully platform to say mean things about other people. Don't post embarrassing photos of others.

➢ Using abusive, insulting, or offensive language.

➢ Yelling, shouting or being verbally aggressive.

➢ Making unprovoked violent physical contact or threatening gestures.

➢ Making negative comments about a person's family, appearance, lifestyle, speech, hair, or culture.

Bullying others is mean and teens must learn to evade and put a stop to bullying behaviors. Half of us at one point have been bullied. I was bullied, teased, and made fun of because my parents divorced, and I spoke "proper American English". Bullying is hurtful and mean spirited. If you are being threatened or bullied on social media or at school, do not harm or injury yourself tell someone. Report it immediately to the teacher, parent, or police. **REPORT IT!** You are loved and important.

How to Stop Bullying

1. Acknowledge that is it wrong to bully others. (Apologize)
2. Identify and stop aggressive behaviors.
3. Talk with a counselor at school or your parents about why you bully others.
4. Learn how to manage your emotions and resolve conflict.
5. Most importantly, get counseling and find out why you want to hurt others.

You need to learn how to self-regulate (control) your attitude and emotions. If you take time to stop and think before you act or speak you will develop good habits.
Your choices will determine the consequences of your behavior.

ANGER MANAGEMENT

A self-assessment can provide insight into your level of anger. The following questions can help you understand why you get so angry and how to stop getting so mad.

Anger Management

1. When does anger become a problem?

Anger becomes a problem when the feelings are too intense, and your expressions and responses are inappropriate. Anger is negative energy that causes violent, abusive, and aggressive physical assaults.

2. What can you do when angry?
   - Take deep breathes.
   - Walk outside.
   - Talk with a counselor and parent.

Peer pressure can be positive or negative and can influence the behavior of others. Starting a "anger management' peer group can bring people together to create positive changes. If you are a good leader you are concerned about others. A caring leader has concern for others and treats them respectfully.

Many teenage activists and role models are famous and making a difference in politics, schools and communities.

Taking a leadership role in high school is a great way to stand out among your peers. Leadership is an important skill that can benefit high school students seeking college admission. As a teen, if you do something meaningful you will find life's purpose. If you embrace compassion and kindness, you will find empathy. If you embrace nonviolent behaviors, create positive changes, and be kind to others, you can be a transformational teen leader.

Chapter 3

Life Skills for Student Success

Teens face many problems and challenges today, such as student drop-out, family problems, substance abuse, racism, peer pressure, vaping, cyber addiction, depression, bullying, self-esteems, and issues related to body image. Many problems can be resolved if teens listen, ask questions, and show respect toward others. Good communication can help solve problems. Good communication and education can prevent student drop-out. Effective communication is the most valuable skill a teen, parent, teacher, or adult can develop to improve relationships.

As a teen, you may not agree with your teacher, caregiver, or parent, but you need to respect them.

RESPECT

Webster's dictionary defines respect as: *"a feeling of deep admiration for someone or something elicited by their abilities, qualities, or achievement."*

Your success in life depends upon showing respect for parents, teachers and adults. Teachers are there to help you succeed, and they care about you. Your parents or caregivers love you and want the best for you. Respecting others is necessary for problem-solving and minimizing conflicts. A teen leader needs to know how to give, gain, and maintain respect. Earning and keeping respect is essential to building peer influence and encouraging others to follow. People respect a leader for their character and actions, not necessarily for their title. A great leader earns respect from peers, family members, teachers, friends, and ordinary everyday people. The acronym for R.E.S.P.E.C.T describes the behavior a leader needs to possess.

Respond: Listen before you speak.
Engage: Be motivated to learn.
Support: Students help other students.
Polite: Say please and thank you.
Empathy: Show concern for others.
Communicate: Repeat what you heard in the
               conversation to avoid
               misunderstandings.
Team: Promote trust.

In America the internet, games, cable television, and social media are blamed for bad manners and the lack of empathy. Respect plays an important role in our daily lives. Respect is positively treating people and encouraging them to share ideas and thoughts. Respect in relationships is honoring and valuing other people and treating them with kindness. Respect and trust are essential in building relationships. Active listening and proper communication are excellent problem-solving skills.

Problem-Solving Skills

This acronym R.E.S.O.L.V.E means: Repeat theproblem. Examine body language and voice tones. Simplify problems. Openly share thoughts and feelings. List your ideas. Validate others. Evaluate the consequences. The problem-solving strategies can help teens improve and build communication skills; improve active listening, and solve-problems effectively. Teens that learn how to control emotions can manage conflict and problems.

R.E.S.O.L.V.E

Repeat: To gain a better understanding of what you heard a person say, you should repeat the information to clear up any misunderstanding. Rephrasing can clarify what has been said.

Examine: Body language and voice tones are an integral part of problem-solving. Use non-threatening body language. Calm voice tones can de-escalate conflicts and prevent violence.

Simplify: State and identify the current problem. Stay focused on the issue. Report all bullying and threatening events.

Openly: Communicate openly and respectfully. Be a good listener and allow others to share their thoughts.
List: Write your expectations and review your weekly performance goals.

Validate: Be open to feedback without judging it as good or bad. Validate people's differences and respect them.

Evaluate: Body language, voice tones, and behaviors are forms of communication. New skills can help you find new ways to problem-solve.

How to Make Good Decisions

It is essential to learn how to make good decisions for a successful academic and personal life.

1. Ask the question: Is it the right thing to do?
2. Mission: Stick to your goals.
3. Distraction: Avoid peer pressure.
4. Data: Get facts and identify problems.
5. Focus Group: Gather four people who are smarter than you.
6. Knowledge: Search out the knowledge you need.
7. Conduct a risk assessment: What are the risks? How will it affect your education and the quality of your life?

Students can be engaged in making powerful, meaningful, and substantive choices, decisions and determinations that affect themselves, peers, communities, and the world. It is important to learn how to make decision that are intentional, not accidental or coincidental. In decision making seek input, data, and knowledge to avoid bad choices. A wrong decision can have a long-term adverse effect on your education and personal life.

Five Conflict Resolution Skills

1. Remain calm: Breathe. Talk without yelling, screaming, and name calling. Monitor body language and voice tones.

2. Express: Say what you mean specifically. Share what you need and want. Be open to feedback.

3. Respect: Speak and treat people like you want to be treated.

4. Listen: Listen with your ears and heart without interrupting. Repeat what you heard to avoid misunderstanding.

5. Area: Use inside voices when at home, school and or in public. You avoid offending people when you use appropriate voice tones.

Conflict resolution skills can improve student and teacher interaction as well as peer-to peer and parent–child interaction.

Chapter 4

Financial Literacy for Career Success

Most parents have never received financial education and therefore, teens don't have training on how to handle their money. Financial literacy is designed to prepare teens for adulthood. When my daughter turned twelve, she learned how to balance a checkbook, fill out a money order, and make bank deposits. Teenagers who are educated about finances can avoid financial problems in the future and develop long-term financial success.

Teenagers who learn how to budget can successfully manage money when they get older. A budget is a guide that can help you monitor your spending and help you save money. A budget allows you to gauge whether you're going in the right direction financially. A budget allows you to control your money instead of your spending habits controlling you. A budget can help you meet your saving goals. A budget is an instrument for setting aside money for savings, investments, vacations, and emergencies.

One key to managing your money is budgeting. I know you are saying, "Dr. Reba, I am a teenager, and I don't have money to manage." Do you receive an allowance for chores? If you receive an allowance or work part-time, you can start saving and watch your savings grow. You can save money in a checking or savings account.

If you learn to save money and live on a budget, you can avoid financial hardships. Budgeting is the simplest form of planned spending. A budget can help you save money for investments, a car, college, shoes, clothes, and emergencies.

A budget can benefit the entire family as they focus on a common goal. A budget can help you prepare for large, unanticipated expenses, i.e., car expenses, an air conditioner or home repairs. A budget tracks monthly income and outgoing expenses, monies coming in and payments going out.

Understanding financial principles and developing money management skills can improve your economic life in the future. Money management and debt elimination are part of financial planning. Discipline in spending and a new way of thinking are both required for financial steadiness. Financial education is critical to building a secure financial future. Economic ignorance will not protect you from the consequences of making poor financial decisions.

In life what you don't know can harm you. If you attend college or a vocational trade school, be aware that credit card companies will send you credit card applications galore. If you are graduating from high school or entering college or a vocational trade school, you don't need credit card debt.

How Credit Scores Affect Your Life

It is important to understand how to build your credit score. In America, credit scores determine if you can purchase a house, rent an apartment, open a business, or purchase a car and so much more. Unfortunately, identity thieves can use your social security number and destroy your credit. Also, unfortunately, some relatives or parents use their child's social security number to open credit card accounts, apply for loans, and rent apartments.

It's a good idea for you, a caregiver, or a parent to check your credit report close to your 16th birthday.

Credit scores are directly tied to lower interest rates. As a real estate broker and former mortgage broker I know that sadly many parents could not obtain a home loan due to low credit scores. According to the three credit-reporting agencies, a person with an 800 to 850 is considered to have an exceptional credit score. A person with a credit score in the range between 700 and 800 is believed to have good credit. A person with a credit score between 500 and 600 is considered to have with poor or low credit score. A borrower with a low credit score between 500 and 600 cannot obtain a home loan and is required to put 20% down.

A borrower with lower credit scores has a higher loan interest rate, and lenders require a more substantial down payment.
Purchase price $150,000
20% down $30,000
Balance of loan $120,000

Exceptional Credit

A borrower with high credit scores has a lower loan interest rate, and a lender requires a smaller down payment.

$150,000
3% down $4,500
Balance of loan

Purchasing a home is the most significant investment most of us will ever make. Before, you buy a house, attend a homebuyer workshop and decide if you want to commit to a thirty-year or fifteen-year mortgage.

Ask yourself these questions

1. Do want a financially stable life?
2. Do you have savings?
3. Do you want a good job, open a business, and have a steady income?
4. Is your income sufficient to purchase a house?

As an adult, you can have the American dream of becoming a home owner, but you must first graduate high school, complete college or vocational or trade program.

In order to purchase a home you need proof that you are employed and that you have a steady income. As a borrower, you must havea sufficient credit rating to secure a personal, home or auto loan. Mortgage lenders use credit rating as an assessment of an individual's creditworthiness. Credit scores can affect your employment opportunities.

Employers and lenders review your credit reports to find out if you pay your bills on time. Credit scores are affected by how manycreditors are paid late, and how many loans were sent off to collection agencies.

The longer you've had established credit, the better it is for your overall credit score. Lenders look at your past payment history and make a decision based on your ability to pay. Too many inquiries on your credit report negatively affect your credit score and may make it appear that you are in financial trouble. It is imperative that your bills are paid on time to improve your credit score. Late payments are the fastest way to destroy your credit rating. In the loan process, mortgage lenders retrieve each borrower's credit report

Empowering students to be Future-Ready" from Experian, Trans Union, and Equifax.

A person can receive a free credit report once a year from AnnualCreditReport.com. The Fair Credit Reporting Act guarantees access to a free credit report from each of the three nationwide reporting agencies--Experian, Equifax, and TransUnion--every twelve months. Credit Karma also offers free credit scores and reports. The most commonly used credit score today is known as a "FICO" score named after the company that developed it, Fair Isaac Corp.

According to FICO, a person's score consists of the following components:

1. Payment History; 35 percent of the score is determined by the payment history and is the single major factor of the FICO score.

2. Length of Credit History; no credit history can be problematic since it shows no recordable payment history; therefore it is vital to establish between one and two years of credit history.

3. Inquiries; a number of recent inquiries can decrease your credit score tremendously.

4. Types of credit include credit cards, mortgage, and auto loans.

A responsible adult keeps control of their finances and maintains an excellent credit score rating. For example: How much money will you save each month? How much money will you require for personal needs? A budget is a simple way to control spending and save money.

There are two significant costs when setting up a budget: fixed expenses or costs and variable expenses or costs. A fixed expense cost is the same amount each month. These bills are usually paid on a regular basis, such as weekly or monthly and include insurance premiums, real estate taxes, car payments, and mortgage or rent payments. A variable expense includes credit card fees and utilities, costs that can change and are somewhat unpredictable. A personal budget is an itemized list of expected income and expenses.

Personal Budget

1. Giving; all charitable giving.

2. Shelter; renting includes rent, heat, lights, telephone, house supplies, appliance repairs, magazines and newspaper subscriptions, and other home-related expenses. If you are buying a home, it includes house payment, interest, insurance, real estate taxes, repairs, and maintenance and other items listed under renting.

3. Food; grocery store items, paper goods, cleaning supplies, pet food, eating out, carry-out items, and school lunches; also may include entertainment.

4. Clothing; purchases, cleaning repairs. These expenses may be divided into a separate budget for each family member.

5. Health; health insurance premiums, medical, dental, and hospital expenses.

6. Education; school supplies, books, college expenses, uniforms, and equipment.

7. Life insurance; all premiums, whether paid monthly, quarterly or annually.

8. Transportation; gas, oil, repairs, license, personal property tax, and insurance; includes car payments or any money set aside to purchase your next car.

9. Personal allowance; each family member needs to spend on hair care, recreation, babysitting, hobbies, cosmetics, children.

10. Vacations; trips, camping, weekend outings, weddings, funerals, and family visits.

11. Credit Card/Debt; payments on monthly expenses.

12. Savings; amounts set aside for future needs.

Budget

Shelter $_____

Food $_____

Clothing $_____

Health $_____

Education $_____

Transportation $_____

Car Payment $_____

Life insurance $_____

Personal allowance $_____

Vacations $_____

Credit Card/ Debt $_____

Tithes/Giving $_____

Savings $_____

Other regular expenses $_____

TOTAL $_____

Monthly Income $_____
Monthly Expenses $_____

Calculate your monthly income minus your expenses and, if your bills exceed your income, you need to change jobs, work a second job, or eliminate items from the budget. Suggestions: take a lunch; eat at home; make coffee at home. You can save money even if you are spending money at the same time; however you will need to make adjustments to the budget.

Most people pay bills using a debit card, but some people pay bills with a check. A debit card is a payment card that makes payment by deducting money directly from a checking account. If you pay by check, this is a step-by-step process to help you fill out the check properly.

Step 1. Write the date on the line at the top right corner. Write the date you intend the

Empowering students to be Future-Ready" check to be cashed. Do not write a postdated check. The bank will cash it, and your account will be overdrawn, and you will pay overdraft fees.

Step 2: Pay to the order of. Write the name of the company of the person that will receive the check.

Step 3: $ In the box write the amount in numbers that you are paying. Ex. 10.00

Step 4: Write the payment amount in words on the line that says *dollars*.

Step 5: The word FOR. Write what the payment is for. Example: rent, insurance.

Step 6: Sign first and last name on the check.

The routing number is a nine-digit number, for the name of the bank or credit union where the account was opened.

The account number is specific to your personal or business account.

The check number is the number of that specific check.

When writing a check you should also complete a check register. If you pay bills by credit or debit card keep track of your spending. Check your credit card and bank statement regularly.

Number	Date	Transaction	Withdrawal	√	Deposit	$

Enter all transactions in your checkbook register. Deposits and withdrawals are called *transactions*.

1. List the number of the check.
2. Write the date of the check.
3. Write the name on the check.
4. In the withdrawal column write the amount.

If you use a checkbook or debit card, you need to fill out a register to enter all

Empowering students to be Future-Ready"
transactions. You need basic addition and subtraction skills to keep a balanced register. Balancing a checkbook means you've recorded all additions (deposits) made to your account and subtractions (withdrawals). Balancing a checkbook lets you know how much money you have in your checking account. We want you to avoid costly mistakes when you start earning money. Knowledge is power, but if you don't use it, it's wasted. Financial literacy can help you enjoy a debt-free and successful future.

Chapter 5

Risk Factors of E-Cigarettes and Vaping Risk

In the United States teens are increasingly using e- cigarettes at an alarming rate. E-cigarettes can lead to nicotine addiction, and also lead to addiction to other drugs. Nicotine addiction and illegal drug use both can cause problems with learning and memory, as well as long-term behavioral impairments including depression, anxiety, and mood disorders.

Electronic cigarettes are also known as e-cigarettes, e-vaporizers, or electronic nicotine delivery systems, are battery-operated devices that people use to inhale an aerosol, which typically contains nicotine (though not always), flavorings, and other chemicals. They can resemble traditional tobacco cigarettes (cig-a-likes), cigars, or pipes, or even everyday items like pens or USB memory sticks. The common nicknames for e-cigarettes are: e-cigs e-hookahs, hookah pens, vapes, and vape pens.

In 2018 a survey found 1 in 5 high school seniors were vaping nicotine. In August, 2019 the U.S. public health officials announced that they were investigating 193 vaping-related respiratory illnesses that were responsible for the deaths of patients in Illinois. As reported the nicotine in e-cigarettes can have several negative health effects, such as lung damage. Chronic nicotine exposure may lead to insulin resistance and type 2 diabetes, although this risk may be offset by the well-known appetite suppressant effects of nicotine. Inhaled nicotine increases heart rate and blood pressure.

Nicotine is highly addictive in its own right, and it may lead to changes in the brain that increase the risk of addiction to other drugs, especially in young people. Nicotine may also impair brain development in adolescents, leading to attention deficit disorder and poor impulse control. These potential harms of nicotine are particularly worrisome in view of soaring rates of e-cigarette use in U.S. teenagers.

Flavored e-cigarettes may pose another health threat. They often contain a chemical compound called diacetyl, which is associated with a rare lung disease called bronchiolitis obliterans that causes permanent damage to the bronchioles (the tiniest airways in the lungs). Adolescent years are times of important brain development. Brain development begins during the growth of the fetus in the womb and continues through childhood until about the age of 25. Nicotine exposure during adolescence and young adulthood can cause addiction and harm the developing brain according to the National Institute on Drug Abuse (NIDA).

Dr. Haley is a former educator and a certified addiction professional with years of experience working at outpatient and residential drug treatment facilities for youth. Teens struggling with drug use were court-ordered to drug rehabilitation. In drug treatment teens learned how to cope with negative emotions and how to resist drug use and cope with triggers or stressful situations and emotions that lead to cravings. In a recent study, The National Institute of Health reported that university students who used e-cigarettes were significantly more likely to have mental health histories of attention-deficit/hyperactivity disorder, posttraumatic stress disorder, gambling disorder, and anxiety, to report low self-esteem, and to endorse traits of impulsivity.

It is noted that illegal drug use and e-cigarettes affects brain. As a teen, the part of the brain that's responsible for decision making and impulse control is not yet fully developed. Therefore, young people are more likely to take risks with their health and safety, including use of nicotine and other drugs. Teens and young adults are also uniquely at risk for the long-term, long-lasting effects of exposing the developing brains to nicotine. These risks include nicotine addiction, mood disorders, and permanent lowering of impulse control. Nicotine also changes the way synapses are formed, which can harm the parts of the brain that control attention and learning.

To further understand the effects of drugs and nicotine on the brain, a functional brain imaging technique is used to measure the changes in nerve cell activation in the brain. The brain is divided into the Central Nervous System (CNS) and Peripheral Nervous System (PNS). The spinal cord, considered the *old* brain, works with the memory portion in the brain and is closely linked to the emotions. Drugs affect and alter the information sent to the brain by manipulating the CNS.

The use of drugs mostly affects the reward and reinforcement pathway of the brain. The pathway has two switches, the on switch wants "more" and the off switch says "stop." The drug activates the brain and tells it to do more drugs, and the stop switch signals when the craving has been fulfilled. This process shuts down the *more* switch. When the pathway is activated through psychoactive drugs, memories of those euphoric feelings are strongly impacted.

Drug addiction and alcoholism impact the security of the home, the solidarity of families, psychological wellness, physical wellbeing, and general family progression. According to the National Institute on Drug Abuse, "alcohol and other drug use among our nation's youth remains a significant public health problem." Adolescents and older teens primarily abuse alcohol and tobacco, followed by marijuana, inhalant substances (such as breathing the fumes of household cleaners, glues and synthetic marijuana ("K2" or "Spice") and prescription medications—particularly opioid pain relievers like Vicodin, and stimulants such as Adderall.

What are the risk factors for drug addiction ?

- Early aggressive behavior
- Poor social skills
- Substance abuse among peers
- Drug availability
- Poverty
- Lack of parental supervision

Problem-solving and conflict resolution skills can minimize the risk of substance abuse and deter students from E- cigarettes use. Addiction affects the entire family and seeking professional can improve the lives of teens and their family members.

Chapter 6

Business Principles for Success

Some teens are starting businesses before they finish high school; others don't want to start their own business, but prefer to work for someone else. For those who want to start a business, I have a few suggestions: woodcraft, real estate, child care, hair salon, social media influencer, PodCaster or one can be a You Tuber. Whatever business you open will require specific skills. Organizational management is a crucial part of business success.

Organizational Management

Organizational management *is the process of organizing, planning, and leading a business.* Organizational management includes the steps for starting a business and can improve an existing business. Organization management skills include improving time management, openly communicating, and listening to others.

The overall goal of a business owner is to ensure the business is thriving. Business owners face many challenges such as finding employees with the same values, locating affordable healthcare and adjusting to consumer changes.

Organizational Management Skills

1. Essentials of Time Management: Time management leads to success in leadership. Don't waste time; be productive and make the most of your life.

2. Effective Business Writing: Effective business writing requires excellent communication skills. Basic principles of writing, grammar and spelling are important.

3. Communicating and Listening: Clear, appropriate communication and listening are critical in solving problems and building relationships.

Empowering students to be Future-Ready"

4.   Effective Facilitation Skills: Public speaking is important in influencing and persuading others to support your cause.

5.   Managing Stress: Eating healthy, resting, avoiding alcohol and drugs can reduce stress and help leaders live a better and healthier life.

These organizational management skills are essential to the success of business owners. Organizational skills can help employees and leaders to get more done. Excellent organization and time management skills increase productivity.

In business, time is money and wasting time is wasting money, so don't spend your time on trivial conversations. Excellent organizational and practical communication skills are necessary to build long-lasting business and personal relationships.

Communication is one of the most successful attributes a leader can possess. A strong leader and business owner should possess clear and concise communication and business writing skills. Organizing and

Empowering students to be Future-Ready"
writing brief e-mails and instant messages
are part of business communication.

Organizational Structure

Organizational structure determines
how roles, power, and responsibilities are
assigned, controlled, and coordinated within
a company. An organizational chart
provides structure for the corporation.

Following is a list of things a person should
know before starting a business.

1. What is the legal structure of the
   organization? LLC, C Corp, S Corp, Not-
   for-Profit?
2. Is the organization a 501C (3) IRS tax
   exempt?
3. Who owns what percent of the
   corporation?
4. Who are the President, Secretary, and
   Treasurer?
5. Who are the board members?
6. Will the board members receive
   compensation?

Empowering students to be Future-Ready"

7. What is the legal purpose of the corporation?

8. Are the board of directors meetings open to the public?

9. Do you have a business plan to present to a bank and investor?

10. Will the common stock be issued or authorized?

11. Do you have an organizational chart?

The organizational chart details the chain of command. It is a way of showing the positions and ranks of the management team. The goal of financial management is to monitor and control the financial resources of the organization. A bookkeeper, an accountant, and chief financial officer are responsible for monitoring, creating budgets, and tracking current and future revenues. The overall fiscal responsibility of an organization is to develop departmental budgets. A corporate budget projects the income and expenses of a specific department to achieve its financial goals.

A written business plan and talking to a group of people that you trust can help you in decision-making and developing a marketing plan. These business principles can help teen entrepreneurs be successful in a business startup. One way to create or find a great idea is to talk with a group of friends. Sometimes getting different opinions and thoughts can help you decide what business you want to start. Good friends share ideas!

Chapter 7

Self -Care Practices and Routines

Negative words and negative attitudes can adversely affect your success; words such as, "you are not good enough, you are not smart, you are ugly, you can't succeed," First, the process of change begins with taking fifteen minutes a day to do positive affirmations. Look in the mirror and say to yourself, "I love you." As you continue to confess your love, for yourself, your self-esteem and self- image will be rebuilt and redefined. It is my belief that we are created in love and when we love self, we will show love and respect to others. Regardless of what people say about you, you must say always say positive things about self. Next, to positively change your thinking associate with peers who are success focus, optimistic, and goal orientated. For example the goals maybe to change attitude, improve grades, or learn a new hobby.

If a person wants different results, he or she must do something different. If an individual continues to do the same things, he or she will ultimately receive the same results. Change demands risk. Many teens resist change and find it difficult to make life adjustments. Fear of the unknown can prevent and hinder you from making positive changes in your life. Identify and recognize your fears, and make a decision to practice self-care and ask for help. Change can be stressful, but it can be positive and provide opportunities to meet new people, generate creativity, and expand your knowledge base. Change is a journey requiring flexibility. The process of change begins in the mind and positive words and a positive attitude can change your future.

Whatever you do in life ask yourself "how will it improve my life?" People come into our lives for a reason, season, or a lifetime. You decide who will be friends. You decide who or what is best for you and your future. If you don't like something change it, and if you can't change it, change your attitude about it.
Take control of your life and make the proper changes to be future- ready.

.

Take control of your life and make the proper changes to be a productive, respectful and successful student and adult. These tips can rebuild self- confidence and help you feel good about self.

Self- Esteem Exercises
1. Forgive yourself for past mistakes and poor choices.
2. Make yourself a priority.

3.   Visualize your life getting better.
4.   Know your value and worth.

5.   Celebrate your accomplishments.
6.   Have a positive attitude.
7.   Read self-help books.
8.   Develop a daily routine of positive affirmations.
9.   Look in the mirror every morning and tell yourself " I love you."
10.   Be open to self-image and attitude changes.

When becomes overwhelming and you feel like you are getting lost. Self-care is the healthiest and loving thing you can do. Self-care is necessary for good mental health and healthy living. Students can be so busy attending school, working or helping to take care of a loved one that they don't crave out time for self. .

Self-care practices and routines can improve your mental health, well-being and productivity.

Self –Care Practices

1.   Take a shower or bath.
2.   Read a good fun book.
3.   Meditate in silence.

4.   Volunteer and give back to your community.
5.   Communicate and spend time with friends.
6.   Turn off your IPAD and Phone.
7.   Exercise and walk for 1 or 2 miles
8.   Get some sleep
9.   Enjoy nature.
10.   Play with a pet.

Stress Reduction Techniques

A balanced school-work-life is created by determining priorities, developing time management skills, and setting priorities and goals. A healthy balance of school, work, and life can help to reduce stress.

Ten Techniques to Reduce Stress

The ten stress-reducing techniques can help you live happier and healthier. When you feel stressed and anxious, consider using these suggestions to relieve stress. Often-times spending time with family and friends can lessen stress and increase happiness.

1.   Prioritize; write down your priorities in numerical order. (order brings balance)
2.   Avoid vaping, cigarettes, alcohol and drugs to eliminate problems.
3.   Use yoga and meditation to help you relax.
4.   Exercise can create a healthy lifestyle.

5. Use friends as support and sounding board.
6. Reduce the noise in your environment by listening to relaxing music.
7. Getting a part-time job can improve your socialization skills and finances.
8. Eat vegetables and fruits and drink plenty of water.
9. Get between six and eight hours of sleep per night to rejuvenate your body and mind.
10. Turn off smart phones (at least for part of the day).

Peer pressure can make you want to be someone you are not. Evaluate your peer groups, friendships, associations, and relationships. Friendship is a two-way street, and each person should be a giver. Friends are supportive and boost each other's self-esteem. If a person does not add value to your life and make you feel good about yourself, end the relationship. Time is more valuable than money and to reach your future you will have to examine every peer relationship.

Spending quality time with family and friend girls increases a sense of belonging. Eating a meal, taking a bike ride, or walking together strengthens a family's bonds. Getting adequate sleep and eating healthy foods are necessary for a healthier lifestyle.

Healthy living requires teens to take some personal time to relax, and do something enjoyable. The COVID -19 lockdown had an impact on the mental health of students and adults. Inform your parent or caregiver if you experience a change in mood, feelings of sadness and hopelessness, or rage. Sharing your feelings with others is a healthy form of self-care.

.

Chapter 8

Impact of Substance Abuse on Families

Addiction is a family disease that poisons marriages, families, children, parents, and grandparents. Drug addiction and alcoholism impact the security of the home, the solidarity of families, psychological wellness, physical wellbeing and general family progression. According to the National Institute on Drug Abuse (NIDA), "every day, more than 115 people in the United States die after overdosing on opioids. The misuse of, and addiction to, opioids including prescription pain relievers, heroin, and synthetic opioids such as fentanyl is a serious national crisis that affects public health, as well as a social and economic welfare concern.

The Center for Disease Control and Prevention estimates that the total "economic burden" of prescription opioid misuse, alone, in the United States is $78.5 billion a year, including the costs of healthcare, lost productivity, and criminal justice involvement." The National Institute on Drug Abuse also estimated 88,000 people (approximately 62,000 men and 26,000 women) die from alcohol-related causes annually, and in addition 64,000 deaths from drug overdoses were estimated in 2016. From 1999 to

Empowering students to be Future-Ready"
2016, more than 630,000 people died from a drug
overdose, and around 66% of the drug overdose
deaths in 2016 involved an opioid. In 2016, the
number of overdose deaths involving opioids}
including prescription opioids and illegal opioids
such as heroin and illicitly manufactured fentanyl)
was 5 times higher than in 1999.

Alcohol and other drug use among our nation's
youth remains a major public health problem in
America. Adolescents and older teens primarily
abuse alcohol and tobacco, followed by marijuana,
inhalant substances such as, breathing the fumes of
household cleaners, glues and synthetic marijuana
"K2" or "Spice" and prescription medications —
particularly opioid pain relievers like Vicodin and
stimulants such as Adderall. I worked as a substance
abuse counselor in a residential facility with male
and female adolescents. They were admitted for
opioids use and smoking marijuana, and K2, and
Spice and truancy from school.

On admission they were extremely agitated
and violent and had hallucinations. Approximately,
95% of the youth had a mental health disorder and
substance abuse disorder and were dually
diagnosed. Many male and females clients were
prescribed Adderall and diagnosed with
Oppositional Defiant Disorder and Conduct
Disorder. Parents don't want to believe that their

child will use drugs, but statistics show drug and alcohol use among teens has increased. School drug prevention programs and drug free awareness campaigns can influence adolescents and teens to avoid drug use.

Scientist researching addiction suggests that environmental and genetic factors increase the risk of addiction. The influence of the home environment is most important in childhood, and family stability can improve childhood education. Research shows that appropriate parental monitoring can reduce future drug use of those prone to marijuana use. Peers that use drugs can influence others to experiment with drugs.

According to the Substance Abuse and Mental Health Service Administration (SAMHSA), frequent marijuana use is associated with decreased attention, poor judgment, social withdrawal and the preoccupation with acquiring marijuana. The results of substance use for adults and adolescents are family relationship problems, criminal behavior, and legal problems. Adolescents and individuals with mental disorders are at greater risk of drug abuse and addiction.

In the most recent study, by Monitoring the Future (MTF), of the behaviors, attitudes, and values of American secondary school students, college

Empowering students to be Future-Ready"
students, and young adults, it was reported that
marijuana and prescription medications are among
the most abused drugs by 8th, 10th and 12th graders.
When a child is found to be using substances, the
family lectures, blames, criticizes and yells to get the
child to change their behavior. The child on the other
hand gets defensive and/or denies that there is any
problem. A child that is using drugs, or drinking, can
have social, family, legal, and/ or, school problems. It
can be easy to focus on the bad habits when
substance use is involved.

In the Journal of Psychoactive Drugs, the
researchers conducted a study that included 65 boys
and 23 girls between the ages of 11 & 17. The
participants were diagnosed with substance use
disorders (SUD), and attended a community drug
and alcohol treatment center. The substance-abusing
adolescents were compared over five psychological
domains of self-concept, anxiety, depression, and
disruptive behavior. The purpose of the study was to
determine if mental health symptoms differed by
gender, in substance abusing adolescents.

The Beck Youth Inventories was used as a part
of the assessment. The findings reported that
teenagers demonstrated higher psychological
problems and those SUD adolescents would have
poor treatment outcomes. Adolescents with pre-
existing anxiety disorders, mood swings, and
conduct disorders were reported to be at a higher

risk of substance use problems. Co-occurring disorders can also be found in adolescents and adults with substance use problems.

These are the following behavioral treatments that have shown promise and that can be effective for adults and adolescents seeking help.

Cognitive-behavioral therapy (CBT): Can be an effective treatment approach to help adults and adolescents with coexisting substance use and mental health problems. CBT is a form of psychotherapy that teaches people strategies to identify and correct problematic behaviors, in order to enhance self-control, stop drug use, and address a range of other problems that often co-occur with them.

Motivational enhancement therapy (MET): A systematic form of intervention designed to produce rapid, internally motivated change; the therapy does not attempt to treat the person, but rather mobilize his or her own internal resources for change and engagement in treatment.

NIDA funded studies suggest that medical marijuana might be associated with decreased prescription use, and overdose of, opioids. The term medical marijuana refers to using the whole, unprocessed marijuana plant, or its basic extracts, to treat symptoms of illness and other conditions. The

Empowering students to be Future-Ready"
scientific study of the chemicals in marijuana is
called cannabinoids and has led to two FDA-
approved medications that contain cannabinoid
chemicals in pill form. Currently, the two main
cannabinoids from the marijuana plant that are of
medical interest are tetrahydrocannabinol (THC) and
Cannabinoids (CBD).

THC can increase appetite and reduce nausea.
THC may also decrease pain, inflammation (swelling
and redness), and muscle control problems. CBD
doesn't make people "high." It may be useful in
reducing pain and inflammation, controlling
epileptic seizures, and possibly even treating mental
illness and addiction. A growing number of states
have legalized medical marijuana and believe that it
may help treat a range of illnesses and symptoms.
However, there is a great debate in our country
regarding the effects of marijuana on the brain of
adolescents.

Adolescents' brains are still maturing, and their
brains are still developing. The use of marijuana, or
any drug, at an early age can have a long-lasting
effect on the brain. Also, marijuana increases the
heart rate, can harm the lungs and may increase the
risk of psychosis in vulnerable individuals.

Is marijuana a gateway drug? The question
that is asked is: Does marijuana lead to more

Empowering students to be Future-Ready"
dangerous and hard drug use? In my opinion and experience, the majority of adult clients state that they began smoking marijuana between the ages of 12 and 13 and research does not support that myth. However, now, adolescents are smoking marijuana at an earlier age.

According to the National Institute on Drug Abuse (NIDA), scientists estimate that genetic factors account for between 40% and 60% of people being vulnerable to addiction. 45% of all deaths in 2015 were related to prescription drug abuse. Individuals are not taking their medicines in the way their doctor prescribed them. In 2010, the number of prescription medicine abusers was 8.76 million, most abused painkillers, tranquilizers, and stimulants.

The initial decision to take drugs is mostly voluntary; people take drugs for various reasons; firstly to make themselves feel better, secondly, curiosity, and because others are doing it, and thirdly, to feel good. Most abused drugs produce a euphoric feeling of intense pleasure and motivate repeat behaviors that are detrimental.

According to the NIDA, the following is a list of the commonly used medical and non-medical drugs in America:

Alcohol - is a depressant and produces sleep and

relief of stress and anxiety. Alcohol consumption can damage the brain and liver, in addition it affects movement coordination, problem solving and decision-making abilities.

Amphetamines, including methamphetamine - these are powerful stimulants that can produce feelings of euphoria and alertness. Ice is the slang for crystallized methamphetamine. The drug is generally taken orally or injected, but can be smoked like crack.

Cannabis - contains chemicals, called cannabinoids that are unique to the cannabis plant. Hash, hash oil and marijuana come from cannabis. Cannabis is usually smoked and alters the sense of self-identity and impairs memory.

Cocaine - is the most powerful stimulant of natural origin. The active stimulant can lead to respiratory problems and severe chest pains. The powder is generally snorted or dissolved in water and injected. Crack cocaine, also known simply as crack, is a free base form of cocaine that can be smoked.

Ecstasy (MDMA) - is called the "club drug" It produces both stimulation and mind-hallucinations. The drugs can be taken orally, sometimes are snorted, but are rarely injected.

Heroin - is a powerful opiate drug that produces euphoria and feelings of relaxation. It slows respiration and can increase the risk of serious infectious diseases, especially when taken intravenously (In several states there is an increase in heroin use).

Inhalants - are a diverse group of substances that includes volatile substances found in many household products, such as lighter fluids, cleaning fluids, and paints that induce mind-altering effects. Inhalants may be sniffed directly from an open container or sniffed from a rag soaked in substances and which is held up to the face.

Lysergic Acid Diethylamide (LSD) - is one of the most potent hallucinogenic drugs known to science. Hallucinogens may elevate heart rates and increase blood pressure and cause distorted thoughts.

Nicotine - is an addictive stimulant found in cigarettes and other forms of tobacco. Tobacco smoke increases a user's risk of cancer, emphysema, bronchial disorders, and cardiovascular disease. (It is reported that by 2050 America will be a non-smoking country)

Prescription medications, and some over-the-counter medications, are increasingly being abused (used for nonmedical purposes). The misuse of prescription painkillers, heroin and fentanyl can be addictive, and in some cases, lethal. Among the most disturbing aspects of this, is the misperception that because physicians prescribe these medications, they are safe even when they are used not as prescribed. Commonly abused classes of prescription drugs include opioid painkillers, stimulants, and depressants.

- Opioids are usually prescribed for pain relief. Opioids include hydrocodone (Vicodin), oxycodone (OxyContin), morphine, fentanyl, and codeine.

- Stimulants: Methylphenidate (Ritalin, Concerta, Focalin, and Metadate) and amphetamines (Adderall, Dexedrine) are stimulants commonly prescribed for attention-deficit hyperactivity disorders.

- Depressants have been identified as downers and promote sleep and reduce anxiety. Benzodiazepines such as Valium and Xanax are used therapeutically to treat anxiety and manage insomnia.

The following is a list of slang words that are used by teens that use drugs. It is very important for parents, grandparents and caregivers to understand the drug lingo. It is a key to monitoring teens for

Empowering students to be Future-Ready"
drug use.

1. MARIJUANA
   Weed, ghanji, thoint, blunt, press, green, upgrade, trees pressure, loud and killer, funny stuff

2. COCAINE
   Coke, white girl, blow where's the lines, white boy, Charlie, dust, flake, freebase, lady, nose candy, powder, rock, rails, snowbirds, toot, white

3. CRACK
   White boy, hard, cats pee, apple jacks

4. METHAMPHETAMINE
   Meth, Ice, blue, belly, crank crystal

5. TRIPLE C: This stands for Coricidin HBP Cough and Cold. "The triple C or CCC is something that we see a lot of.

If a teen, and or, a loved one, need substance abuse treatment help is available. There are many detoxification centers and substance abuse treatment facilities that use customized treatments for substance abuse, mental health or behavioral issues.

There are two types of addictions substance and behavioral:

The Diagnostic and Statistical Manual of Mental Disorders uses substance abuse to refer to both substance abuse and dependence. The treatment for drugs is intended to help addicted individuals stop compulsive drug seeking and use. Treatment can occur in an outpatient or a residential setting.

Behavioral therapy is an umbrella term for types of therapy that treat mental health disorders. It seeks to identify and help change potentially self-destructive or unhealthy behaviors. It functions on the idea that all behaviors are learned, and that unhealthy behaviors can be changed.

Disruptive behavior disorders include two similar disorders, oppositional defiant disorder (ODD) and conduct disorder (CD). Common symptoms occurring in children with these disorders include; defiance of authority figures, angry outbursts, and other antisocial behaviors such as lying and stealing. Unfortunately, any substance-abusing children grow up to be chemically dependents adults. Most youth are diagnosed with both a mental health and substance abuse disorder, and are dually diagnosed and treated for co-occurring disorders.

There are various treatment programs that offer residential treatment for men, women, and adolescents for 28 days, 90 days, 120 days and 365 days. It is reported that long-term residential treatment may be more beneficial and have more positive treatment outcomes. For many people, treatment may involve multiple treatment episodes, aftercare, and regular monitoring.

Outpatient treatment is considered nonresidential and allows patients to maintain a regular life, live at home, often work, and come to a clinic for treatment. Patients are able to maintain their privacy and return home daily. During substance abuse treatment, teens and families should develop a relapse prevention plan and identify common triggers of relapse. The following list describes the symptoms that can lead to substance use.

1.   Argumentativeness – Arguing about small and ridiculous points of view, indicating the need to always be right. So, you look for an excuse to get high.

2.   Cockiness – Got it made. I do not need to go to church or recovery meetings.

3.   Complacency – Using drugs or drinking

Empowering students to be Future-Ready"
alcohol was not on my mind. It can be
dangerous not to attend self-help meetings
and stay busy.

4.   Depression – Unreasonable and unaccountable
      feelings of despair may occur in cycles, and it
      should be dealt with and talked about to share
      feelings.

5.   Dishonesty –This begins with a pattern of
      unnecessary little lies and deceits with   family
      and friends.

6.   Expecting too much from others - I've changed,
      why hasn't everyone else?

7.   Exhaustion - Allowing yourself to become
      overly tired or in poor health. Feel bad
      enough, and you might begin to think a fix
      or drink could not make it worst.

8.   Forgetting Gratitude – It is good to remember
      where you started from and how much life is
      better today, now that you are sober.

9.   Frustration – At people and also because
      things may not be going your way.

10.   Impatience - Things are not happening   fast
      enough, or others are not doing what you think

Empowering students to be Future-Ready"
that they should, or want them to do.

11. It can't happen to me - Dangerous
    thinking. It can happen to you.

12. Letting up on disciplines - You cannot   afford
    to be bored. Stay busy.

13. Loneliness - Never get too Hungry, Angry,
    Tired or Lonely (HALT)

14. Omnipotence – Feeling that you have all the
    answers and your way is the only way to think.

15. Self-Pity - Why do these things always
    happen to me? Why must I be an addict?

16. Spiritual – Lack of spiritual
    acknowledgment. Find a God of your
    understanding to   strengthen your
    recovery.

17. Wanting too much - Happiness is not having
    what you want, but wanting what you have.
    Find contentment.

> Three Types of Relapse

When someone is in recovery from his or her addiction, they should monitor their emotions, and mental and physical condition to prevent relapses.

1.   Emotional: Anxiety, defensiveness, mood swings, isolation and poor sleeping or eating habits.

2.   Mental: Having negative thoughts about people, places, and things. Hanging out with old friends, listening to the same old music and being dishonest, are risk factors.

3.   Physical: Not taking care of your personal hygiene or your living conditions and your weight changes.

Relapse Prevention Strategies

It is important to learn about, and how to use relapse prevention techniques. Relapse prevention is a cognitive-behavioral approach with the goal of identifying and preventing high-risk situations. Recovery requires a change in thought and behavior.

- Stress
- Anger

- Neglecting recovery goals
- Isolation
- Meditation
- Praying
- Jogging
- Journal (writing)

Good communication is the key to solving problems. The seven best practices for communication and problem solving were developed to minimize conflict and strengthen family closeness:

1. Repeat: To gain a better understanding of what you heard, repeat the information to clear up any misunderstanding. Rephrasing can clarify what has been said.

2. Examine: Body language and voice tones are an integral part of problem solving.
Use non-threatening body language and calm voice tones.

3. Simplify: State and identify the current problem. Stay focused on the issue and behavior. Do not bring up past issues and problems.

4. Openly: Tell each other how you feel and do not hesitate to share your feelings. Share your needs and be a good listener.

5. List: List your boundaries and expectations. Write down new ideas and your solutions to the problem. Brainstorm together and find workable solutions.

6. Validate: Be open to feedback, without judging it as good or bad. Validate and acknowledge each other's contributions to solving the problem.

7. Evaluate: Body language, voice tones, and behavior. New responses can help you find new ways to solve problems. Be empathic, respectful and civil.

The list of interventions, techniques, and advice families and teens cope with the addiction and abrupt changes in life circumstances. The family addiction and family stress causes members to become angry, anxious and stressed. The high level of stress within the family can causes teens and/or adults to use drugs. Often, families cope with addiction in unhealthy ways, such as by living in denial about the addiction or by following behind their loved one, picking up pieces. Family therapy is beneficial to patients and the families of teens or adults in drug treatment.

Empowering students to be Future-Ready"

Conclusion

Leadership Principles for Teens —
Empowering students to be Future-Ready is
written to prepare students for life events and
give them the skills to thrive in the future. In
the United States teens need an education,
college, or a trade skill to escape poverty. The
techniques, methods, and life skills offer
guidance to improve students' lives in school
and beyond.

As a student the principles can improve
decision- making and problem-solving. The
business and financial principles can help you
start a business, develop a budget, and
manage money. The social and work manners
and etiquettes can help you obtain a job and
succeed in life. The principles can help you
improve emotional learning skills to improve
your life. The communication, problem solving
and conflict resolution skills make you an
effective peer and adult leader. The list of risk
factor of vaping and drug use can deter you
from continued use. This book is designed to
guide you to succeed in life, make better
decisions, and finish school and further your

Empowering students to be Future-Ready"
education. If you apply the principles in this
book you can reach goals, start a business, and
finish school. Education is key in preventing
and eliminating poverty.

Empowering students to be Future-Ready"

Empowering students to be Future-Ready"

Bibliography

Monitoring the Future (MTF)
http://monitoringthefuture.org/

Substance Abuse and Mental Health Service
Administration (SAMHSA)
https://www.samhsa.gov

The Center for Disease Control and Prevention
https://www.cdc.gov/

The Journal of Psychoactive Drugs

http://www.journalofpsychoactivedrugs.com/a
rticles.html

The National Institute of Drugs Abuse (NIDA)
https://www.drugabuse.gov/

The National Institute of Mental Health
https://www.nimh.nih.gov/health/statistics/ind
ex.shtml

U.S. Census Bureau (2012) retrieved February
2019 from U.S. Census bureau Online
https://www.census.gov/

Empowering students to be Future-Ready"

About the Author

Dr. Reba Haley is a former educator in the public and private schools and colleges. She is a multi-gifted motivational speaker and trainer, lecturer, consultant, adviser and business owner. She is also an addiction therapist that works in the U.S. addressing the opioid crisis. She is also a substance abuse professional and conducts drug and alcohol assessments for employees who violate the Department of Transportation drug and alcohol policy. In addition, she is the president of Insight Consulting International Group, Inc a minority business enterprise (MBE) certificate holder, an encompassing consulting and training firm in Tampa, Florida.

She is a native of Detroit earned an associate degree from Wayne County Community College, a Bachelor's Degree in psychology at the University of North Carolina Charlotte, a Master's Degree in addiction counseling, and a Doctoral Degree in counseling from Grand Canyon University and St Thomas Christian College. She has several state and local certifications and licenses. She is the owner of several businesses.

She is an ordained minister and has been married for twenty-four years and has two children. Dr. Reba had many obstacles in her life as a teenager, but her faith in God, and her grandmother's inspiration motivated her to finish school. Uplift You is a mentoring program that she begin to help students be better. She mentors young girls about positive self-image and helps to build self- esteem, and foster independence.